CONTENTS

A WORLD OF TREASURE

The world is full of hidden treasure. Buried under the ground, hidden away in secret spots or locked away in tombs, it is lying there, waiting for somebody to find it.

▲ This beautiful sculpture of a bird comes from ancient Syria. It is made of gold, copper and blue gemstones.

The rulers of early civilizations liked to own lots of gold and jewels. Riches made them feel that they were special. But their wealth often made other people want to steal it. So, the kings and queens hid away their treasure and when they died they took their riches to their graves with them.

▶ Howard Carter opens the coffin of Tutankhamun, taking care not to destroy any of the treasures buried within.

◀ This bull's head is part of a harp found in the city of Ur in Mesopotamia. It is 5,000 years old (see page 6).

Not all treasure was buried to hide it. Sometimes it was dropped or lost by mistake. Other times, volcanoes or earthquakes buried whole towns and cities – along with their treasures. Pirates often hid their stolen loot, but many got caught and hanged before they could go back and find it. Sometimes buccaneers (pirates or adventurers) lost the treasure maps that they'd drawn to show them where to dig! Most hidden treasure is dug up soon after it is buried. But a lot more isn't found and is still hidden to this very day. Who knows who will find it?

THE OLDEST TREASURE

▲ This section of the royal flag of Ur shows a musician playing to people at a feast.

Some of the oldest treasure in the world was found in Ur, an ancient city in Mesopotamia (now called Iraq). Five thousand years ago, Ur was one of the most important cities in the world. Then it was taken over by enemy armies. They stole its treasures and left the empty city to fall to pieces.

In 1922, an archaeologist called Leonard Woolley decided to search for Ur's long-lost treasures. For nearly five years he worked, digging up one grave after another and finding nothing. Finally he decided that the treasure must have been stolen long ago. Then, just as he was about to give up, he hit gold!

▼ The king's guards in Ur carried daggers like these. The dagger cover is made of pure gold.

One day, Woolley found an amazing tomb. Buried in it was one of the queens of Ur. The queen's bones were still in the tomb. There was a headdress which had gold rings, leaves and flowers. The queen's black wig was covered with gold leaves too, and these were tipped with lovely reddish-white stones.

There was a wig that had a comb still in it and was decorated with golden flowers. Nearby were golden earrings and huge necklaces made of gold, silver and beautiful stones. Outside the tomb, Woolley found some writing. He found out that it said 'Pu-abi', which was the name of the queen.

A FIELD OF TREASURE

In 1942, an English farmer found treasure buried in his field in Mildenhall, England. There were silver dishes, spoons, bowls and drinking cups. These items had once belonged to a Christian Roman general called Lupicinus. His family probably buried it in a hurry some time in AD 370. Perhaps they were trying to escape from an attack by Anglo-Saxons (an old English people) and, for some reason, they couldn't come back to fetch their belongings.

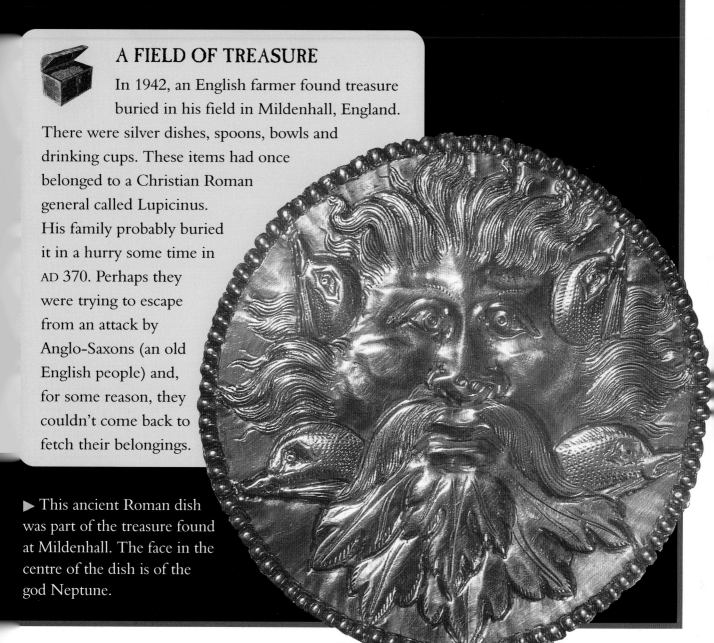

▶ This ancient Roman dish was part of the treasure found at Mildenhall. The face in the centre of the dish is of the god Neptune.

▲ Some of Tutankhamun's golden rings were decorated with scarab beetles.

TREASURES OF THE PHARAOHS

The pharaohs (kings) of ancient Egypt were very rich. When they died, they were buried in huge tombs called pyramids. All their treasures were buried with them so they would be just as rich in the next life too.

But tomb robbers were always breaking into the pyramids to steal the treasures. So the pharaohs started building their tombs in a secret and mysterious place now known as the Valley of the Kings.

▼ Many ancient Egyptian kings were buried in the Valley of the Kings.

Some of the tombs were built high up in the steep rocks where tomb robbers could not get to them. They had lots of secret paths leading nowhere to put off robbers, and the burial chambers were built to look as if they were only half-finished and held no riches. But thieves still found their way in and stole a lot of the pharaohs' treasures.

One tomb that robbers didn't find was that of the pharaoh Tutankhamun. On 6 November 1922, the archaeologist Howard Carter found a staircase that led down into the sand to a strange door. A second pathway led to another door and to Tutankhamun's tomb. The treasure inside it was so rich and beautiful that nobody had ever seen anything like it before.

▲ The back of Tutankhamun's throne shows him talking to his wife, Queen Ankhsenamun.

TUTANKHAMUN'S TOMB TREASURE

When Carter went into the great pharaoh's tomb, he found four rooms filled with treasure. There was a golden throne and furniture, model boats, musical instruments, jewellery and weapons – even a golden chariot that the pharaoh would have been carried round in. In the burial chamber was Tutankhamun's coffin. The king's body was wrapped in bandages dotted with jewels. On his face was a golden mask.

VIKING HOARDS

▲ These jewelled, gold pyramids were once part of a Viking's sword.

Not everyone who finds treasure wants to become rich from it. Edith Pretty owned some land in Sutton Hoo, a village in Suffolk, England, and often wondered what was under the great piles of earth in her fields.

In 1938, archaeologists started digging in the smaller piles. They found a few pieces of pottery and some bones. This told them that Mrs Pretty's fields were once burial grounds that had belonged to the Vikings – pirates who travelled to Britian from Scandinavia.

BURIED FROM THE BLITZ

Soon after the Second World War began, Mrs Pretty's treasures had to be buried yet again. This time they were put in a secret tunnel under the streets of London so that they would not get damaged by wartime bombs.

◀ These gold coins were found at Sutton Hoo. No one knows for sure who their Viking owner was.

A year later, the archaeologists started digging in the biggest pile of all. Soon they had dug up what was once a giant boat. The wood had fallen to pieces but the ancient nails were still in place, showing what shape the boat had once been. In the middle of the boat was a burial chamber. It was full of amazing treasure from the time of the Vikings.

This Viking helmet from Sutton Hoo is made of gold and silver. It probably belonged to a powerful warrior.

There were silver dishes, golden jewels, bowls, spoons, a purse full of golden coins and many other beautiful and expensive things. Mrs Pretty gave all the treasure of Sutton Hoo to museums. She wanted everyone to be able to enjoy it and to learn more about the Vikings.

WHO WAS BURIED IN SUTTON HOO?

There were no bodies in the ship. Perhaps they had rotted away. But one of the jewels that was found (a sceptre) probably belonged to a king, so maybe he was buried there. Some of the coins found were made in AD 625, the same year that the ruler Raedwald died. Sutton Hoo might be this famous Viking's grave.

11

GOLDEN CANNONBALLS

▲ This picture shows Genghis Khan fighting his enemies.

Genghis Khan was the first great ruler of the Mongol empire. He lived in the 12th century BC. With his armies he conquered many lands. As they travelled from place to place, he and his family lived in a yurt (a tent). The tent was covered with stolen treasures – silks, furs, silver bowls and jewel-covered swords.

Eventually, Genghis Khan's empire stretched from China to the River Dnieper in Europe. Wherever he went, Genghis Khan made the people give up their hidden treasures. Some of the stolen treasure was used to decorate his tent. The rest was hidden away, and a lot of it has never been seen since.

► This model is wearing clothes like those worn by wealthy Mongolian women around the time of Genghis Khan.

During his battles, Genghis Khan sometimes ran out of ammunition to fire from his cannons. Then he would order his soldiers to melt some of his gold and turn it into cannonballs. His enemies never knew they were being attacked with treasure. And many of the golden cannonballs still lie hidden in fields and forests to this very day.

▲ This silver cup was found in a Mongolian khan's (ruler's) tomb. It is about 700 years old.

▼ The model chariot is made of pure gold and still shines as if it was brand-new.

MORE STOLEN TREASURE

In 1877, a load of golden objects was found by the River Oxus in Afghanistan. Traders and thieves tried to get the treasure across the Khyber Pass and into India. But it ended up in the hands of an important British soldier who gave it to the British Museum. The treasure included jewellery, dishes and a tiny chariot with four horses. It is about 2,500 years old. The loot had once belonged to Persians, who were well-known for making beautiful things from gold.

7

THE GOLDEN CITY

▲ This is the golden model found near Lake Guatavita. It shows a king surrounded by his men.

▼ The mysterious Lake Guatavita lies in Colombia, a country in South America. Who knows what treasures lie hidden in its waters?

Spanish soldiers travelled to Central and South America in the early 1500s. They had heard stories of a city of gold called El Dorado. Some wanted to find this place and take its treasures back to their own country. Many greedy people looked for the city, but none of them found it. Was the legend true?

We now know that the ancient story was not about a city, but a man. He was king of the Muisca people, who lived high in the Andes Mountains near Lake Guatavita. Every year, in a special ceremony, the king was covered in gold dust. He then dived from a boat into the lake to show how much he respected (honoured) the lake god.

In 1969, two farmers found something really amazing in a cave by Lake Guatavita. It was a golden model of the great king on his boat, with the men who rowed his boat around him. The story of El Dorado seemed to be true after all. Since then people have tried and failed to empty the lake. Who knows what golden treasures still lie in the water where the Muisca dropped them?

GOLD FOR A KING

The English explorer Sir Walter Raleigh tried and failed to find El Dorado for King James I. In 1617, he led a group of travellers to find the famous city in Guiana, South America.

▲ When Sir Walter Raleigh returned to England without any treasure, the King ordered soldiers to cut his head off!

PIRATE TREASURE

Pirates were the most famous treasure hunters of all. For thousands of years, these sea robbers travelled the world's oceans, attacking any ship they came across. They stole jewels such as pearls, silver, gold and emeralds. They also took expensive paintings, golden crosses covered with jewels and all kinds of weapons.

▲ These gold coins were found near a ship wrecked in Uruguay, South America. No one knows who they belonged to.

Most pirates spent their share of the loot (stolen treasure) as soon as they got it. But some buried theirs in secret places. The pirate Captain Kidd was said to have hidden his treasure on Gardiners Island on the East Coast of America. He was finally caught and taken to England. He offered a huge amount of treasure to the people that kept him prisoner to set him free. But everyone thought he was telling a lie to save himself, and the unlucky pirate was hanged in May 1701.

► Captain Kidd watches his pirates dig a hole to hide his treasure.

Some people think that his treasure is still hidden on the island. Others think that he really was lying and had no treasure at all. Perhaps we will never find out what really happened. It's always hard to work out who is telling the truth about buried treasure. Everyone wants to find it themselves and they want to stop other people from finding it first!

BLACKBEARD'S TREASURE

The famous pirate Blackbeard is believed to have hidden riches on Plum Island near the coast of North America. 'Only two people know where my treasure is,' he liked to say, 'me and the Devil. He who lives the longest can keep it all.'

◄ Plum Island lies just off the coast of New York, USA. It is named after the many plum trees that grow there.

TREASURE ISLAND

The island of Cocos near Costa Rica is a real treasure island. During the 1600s and 1700s, it was used as a place to hide by many pirates. Most of them were trying not to be caught after they'd broken the law. William Thompson was a well-known Scottish pirate who was said to have buried treasure there.

▲ Long John Silver is one of the most famous pirates in the world. But he did not really exist. He was a character in the book, *Treasure Island*.

▼ The churches on the small island of Gozo in the Mediterranean Sea are said to be full of treasures.

THE GOLDEN COW OF GOZO

A farmer on the small Mediterranean island of Gozo once found a model of a golden cow in his field. He sold it to a local trader who then hid it. When the person in charge of the island heard about the treasure he told the trader that he must give it up. But the man said he would not and was sent to prison. He died in jail without telling anyone where the golden cow was hidden. Since then, the people of Gozo have looked for it, but have never been able to find it.

In 1823, rich Spanish families from Lima in Peru believed that they were going to be attacked and robbed by local people. They asked Thompson to take them to safety on his ship, the *Mary Dear*. Thompson and his men agreed.

But when they saw the great riches belonging to the Spaniards, Thompson's men changed their minds. As soon as they were out to sea they killed the Spaniards and threw their bodies over the side. Then they sailed to Cocos Island to hide the treasure. Some time later, the pirates were caught and all were hanged, apart from Thompson who escaped. But he had travelled a long way from his treasures to avoid capture and was too poor to go back and find them.

Over the years many people have tried to find his riches, but nobody has succeeded.

▲ In the past, people liked to take gold nuggets with them on sea journeys. They were easy to carry and hide.

THE DUTCHMEN'S MINE

There is a secret gold mine in the Superstition Mountains of Arizona, USA. The story says that there is so much gold in it that when you tap on the walls, the nuggets just fall into your hands. The Native American Apaches were the first to find the gold in the mountains. They told the Spaniards about the riches when Europeans first visited Arizona in the 1700s.

GOLD RUSH

In 1848, a man called John Marshall found a piece of gold in a Californian river. The news caused a wild rush, as people from all over the world hurried to California to find the treasure. This search for gold is still known to this very day as the California Gold Rush.

▲ Golden nuggets like this one are said to be hidden in Dutchmen's Mine in Arizona.

▲ A man searches for gold during the California Gold Rush. He swills pebbles around in a pan hoping to find a gold nugget among them.

◀ The fierce sun makes digging for gold in the Superstition Mountains hard and thirsty work.

Soon, many people were trying to find the mine. The gold hunters began to fight with each other. The Apaches became angry. The treasure hunters were spoiling their land, so they did everything they could to keep the secret of the mine from them.

Two of the men looking for the gold were German, but the locals thought they were Dutch. They gave the mine its name, Dutchmen's Mine. The Germans did find some gold, but the Apaches then hid the opening to the mine with rocks. Later, an earthquake closed off the mine forever. But, even today, treasure hunters are still looking for the gold. They still dream of great riches.

AFRICAN GOLD

One night in 1892 King Lobengula of Matebeleland in Africa went on a secret journey with a huge amount of gold, ivory and diamonds. He knew that the British were going to attack his land and he wanted to make sure no one stole his riches.

▲ King Lobengula of Matabeleland owned gold, ivory and diamonds from his own mines.

▶ This golden head was once part of a stool that belonged to an African emperor.

The only people who went with Lobengula were a man called John Jacobs, four chiefs and some warriors. The warriors buried the treasure, and when they had finished Lobengula told the chiefs to kill them. Now only six people knew where the riches were hidden.

Lobengula died on the run, while hiding from the British. But John Jacobs never forgot Lobengula's treasure, and on his deathbed he told a friend called Lloyd Ellis about it.

▲ This is what diamonds look like when they are dug out of a mine. Later, they are cut to give them a neat shape.

Ellis travelled all around Matebeleland looking for one of the chiefs who knew where the treasure was buried. Eventually, he found an old man who was said to be one of Lobengula's men. But the old chief had lost his memory long before and couldn't help him. Ellis returned home poor, leaving Lobengula's gold for somebody else to discover. No one has managed to find it yet.

THE COAST OF GOLD

West Africa used to be rich in gold. Hundreds of years ago, African gold was sent across the Sahara Desert, where traders gave it to people in return for salt, spices and perfumes. Soon Portuguese, English, French and Dutch traders were heading for West Africa to find gold for themselves. They named it 'The Gold Coast'.

NAZI LOOT

▲ This American soldier is inspecting some Italian jewellery from the 1500s. The Nazis had stolen it from Paris, France.

During the 1930s the German leader, Hitler, ordered his soldiers to take over Europe. As his troops marched into one country after another, they were told to steal all the art and treasures they could find and send them back to Germany. By 1939, many countries were at war with Germany to try to stop Hitler from taking over Europe.

When the Nazis realized they were losing the war, most of the stolen art treasures were hidden away. Trucks, tanks and even carts were used to carry the stolen goods up mountain paths to secret salt mines near the village of Alt Ausse in Austria. There the art treasures were locked in huge caves.

◄ This famous picture of water lilies, by the French artist Monet, was stolen by the Nazis. It was given back to its owner 50 years after the Second World War.

▲ This is part of a huge hoard of silver stolen by the Nazis. It is being sold after it was found hidden in salt mines in Germany.

ART COLLECTOR GOERING

Herman Goering was a very important German soldier. His love of art was even stronger than Hitler's. Whenever his men went to a museum, a church or an art gallery to steal treasures, Goering always made sure that he took some of the pieces for himself.

In France alone, 21,000 paintings were stolen. After the war, thousands of paintings, drawings, models, books, pieces of furniture and other expensive objects were found in the caves. Before they left to escape back to Germany, the German officers had ordered the Austrian workmen to blow up the mines. But luckily the workmen refused to destroy these amazing treasures. That way some of the greatest works of art in the world were saved.

BURIED-TREASURE FACTS

Here is a selection of interesting facts and figures about buried treasure.

Gold

Gold was one of the first metals to be turned into tools and decorations by humans. It is soft and easy to shape. It does not lose its colour and it keeps its shine, even when buried for ages.

▼ This statue from the ancient city of Ur shows a ram in a bush. It was made about 5,000 years ago.

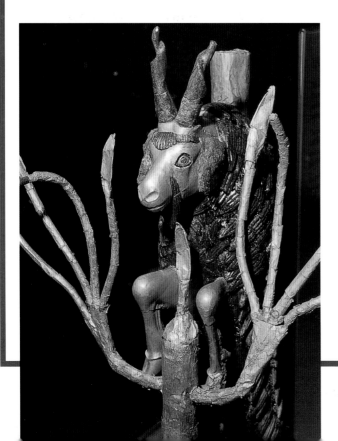

Treasure story

Buried treasure appears in many of the world's myths and legends. In the story, the *Arabian Nights*, a thief called Aladdin finds a cave full of buried treasure. In another story, Sinbad the sailor falls into a valley full of diamonds and is rescued by a giant bird. In ancient Greek stories, a young prince called Agamedes builds a secret room for a king's treasure, then steals it himself.

The greatest treasure in the world

When the Spanish led by Francisco Pizarro attacked the Inca people of Peru during the 1500s, they put the Inca king in prison and asked for money to set him free. The Incas sent Pizarro huge amounts of gold. It was the greatest treasure the world had ever seen. But Pizarro got tired of waiting for all the gold and left. The Incas left some of the treasure in the jungle, and some of it is still there today.

Treasure trove

According to the law, people in England have to tell the police if they find treasure. If they do, they are paid what the treasure is worth. But if they keep the treasure for some time, they won't get as much money.

Treasure Island

The Scottish author Robert Louis Stevenson wrote the most famous book about buried treasure. It is called *Treasure Island* and some say the author wrote it about the legend of Cocos Island (see page 18). Stevenson is thought to have said that 'a man who had not hunted for treasure as a boy was never a child'.

Ghostly guardians

According to folklore, many treasures are looked after by ghosts. The treasure in Chiddingly Place, a grand old house in Sussex, England, is looked after by the ghost of a black hen. Once it attacked a man who was trying to steal it and made him go mad.

Dragons' pearls

In Persian stories, buried treasure is often looked after by dragons. Kings or brave warriors always try to kill the dragons and steal their treasure. In a Chinese story, a farmer finds a very expensive pearl buried outside his house. When he swallows it by mistake, the farmer turns into a dragon.

▲ This golden necklace belonged to Queen Ahhotep Dra Abu'l-Naga in ancient Egypt. It was a present from her sons.

The strangest map

The strangest map in the world was drawn by a pirate called Olivier le Vasseur in the 1700s. When he was about to be hanged, le Vasseur threw the map into the crowd and shouted, 'my treasures to the person who can find them'. But the directions were written so that they were hard to read. No one could work out what the map said and people are still puzzling over it to this day.

Treasure coast

The coast around the Gulf of Mexico is rich in buried treasure. Many Spanish ships are said to have run into its rocky coastline. A famous pirate called Lafitte is also said to have hidden three treasures in the area, although no one has managed to find them.

BURIED-TREASURE WORDS

This glossary explains some words used in this book that you might not have seen before.

Afghanistan
A country in Central Asia.

Ammunition
Items such as bullets and shells that are fired from guns or cannons.

Andes Mountains
A group of mountains in South America.

Apaches
Native Americans from New Mexico and south-western America.

Archaeologist
Someone who studies the past by looking at buried remains of houses, tools and clothes.

Blackbeard
A very famous pirate whose real name may have been Edward Teach. His favourite joke was turning off the lights during dinner and firing off guns under the table. Blackbeard took over a ship with 40 guns and travelled around the coast of America robbing people and causing trouble.

Burial chamber
A special place, often underground or deep inside buildings, where people and their belongings are buried.

◀ Tutankhamun's death mask shows him wearing a beard and the headdress of a king.

▶ These silver spoons from the treasure found in Mildenhall, England, (see page 7) have handles shaped like dolphins. They were made 1,600 years ago when people believed that dophins brought them good luck.

Central America
A big area of land that joins North and South America.

Chariot
A two-wheeled vehicle often pulled by horses.

Devil
In some religions the Devil is the character who stands for everything that is bad or evil.

Gozo
A small island in the Mediterranean Sea.

Hitler
An Austrian who ruled Germany in the 1930s. He believed that true Germans were better than other people, such as Jews and gypsies. He murdered the people he didn't like, as well as trying to take over Europe.

Hoard
A store of something, such as golden coins or jewels.

Loot
Treasure that has been stolen from somebody.

Mediterranean Sea
A great sea between Europe and North Africa.

Mine
A mine is dug into the ground so that people can get at the natural deposits that lie in the earth, such as coal or gold.

Mongol
A person born in Mongolia, a huge region in Central Asia.

Next life
Many people across the world believe that when they die, they will have another life, the next life, in a different place or time.

Nuggets
Lumps of gold, silver or platinum that are found in the earth.

Pirates
Men and women who travel the seas robbing other sailors and stealing ships and boats.

Salt mine
A place where salt can be dug out of the ground.

Scarab beetle
A big beetle that the ancient Egyptians believed to be sacred.

Sceptre
A rod held by a king or queen. Usually made of gold and covered in jewels, it is a symbol of the ruler's power.

Tomb
An area, usually underground, where dead people are buried.

Vikings
Vikings were pirates from northern Europe who raided many countries, including Great Britain, and settled in them.

BURIED-TREASURE PROJECTS

If you want to find out more about buried treasure, here are some ideas for projects.

LOOKING FOR BURIED TREASURE

It is quite easy, and great fun, to make your own guide to buried treasure in your area. First, find out if there are any local stories about buried treasure. Check in your library to see if they have any information. Don't forget to look at books, magazines and the Internet. Libraries also keep old local papers that you can look at. Your tourist office, if you have one, might also have maps and information showing old buildings, castles or houses. Old buildings often have stories about treasure linked to them.

Once you have decided what stories you are going to have in your guide, you can write or type them up. You can also add any photographs of the sites you are writing about. You can decorate your guide too.

▲ This golden belt buckle was once used by a Viking warrior in the 1200s.

YOUR OWN TREASURE HUNT

Treasure hunting can be a very good game, especially if it is played in a big area. Deciding how to do it is often as much fun as the game itself. First of all tell an adult what you are planning to do.

Then, if they are happy for you to do the hunt, decide what the treasure is going to be – sweets, a book or a toy perhaps. Put the treasure in a box and close the lid. Choose a good place for your 'treasure chest' and hide it. Now draw a map, marking the treasure spot with an X. Then add a few landmarks, like shops, phone boxes or a garage, so that the people on the hunt have an idea of where to go.

BURIED TREASURE ON THE WEB

If you have access to the Internet, you can search for sites about buried treasure. Here are a few buried treasure websites to try:

http://www.activemind.com/ Mysterious/
Look through this site for buried treasure mysteries.

http://www.bio.umass.edu/biology/ conn.river/kidd.htm/
Find out more about Captain Kidd's buried treasure (see page 16).

Now give your friends your map and see if they can work out where you have hidden the prize! You can take it in turns to hide the treasure and draw the map for each other.

▶ The jewellery worn by Queen Shubad of Ur was made more than 4,500 years ago. Who knows what other treasures from that time still lie hidden?

INDEX